Trouble-Free Transitions for New Teachers

Middle School and High School Levels

Kimberly T. Strike

Rowman & Littlefield Education
Lanham, Maryland • Toronto • Oxford
2006

Published in the United States of America
by Rowman & Littlefield Education
A Division of Rowman & Littlefield Publishers, Inc.
A wholly owned subsidiary of The Rowman & Littlefield
Publishing Group, Inc.
4501 Forbes Boulevard, Suite 200, Lanham, Maryland 20706
www.rowmaneducation.com

PO Box 317
Oxford
OX2 9RU, UK

Copyright © 2006 by Kimberly T. Strike

All rights reserved. No part of this publication may be reproduced, stored in a retrieval system, or transmitted in any form or by any means, electronic, mechanical, photocopying, recording, or otherwise, without the prior permission of the publisher.

British Library Cataloguing in Publication Information Available

Library of Congress Cataloging-in-Publication Data
Strike, Kimberly T., 1966-
  Trouble-free transitions for new teachers : middle school and high school levels / Kimberly T. Strike.
      p. cm.
  Includes bibliographical references.
  ISBN-13: 978-1-57886-415-7 (pbk. : alk. paper)
  ISBN-10: 1-57886-415-1 (pbk. : alk. paper)
  1. First year teachers—Handbooks, manuals, etc. 2. Middle school teaching—Handbooks, manuals, etc. 3. High school teaching—Handbooks, manuals, etc. I. Title.
  LB2844.1.N4.S822 2006
  373.11—dc22   2006012681

∞^{TM} The paper used in this publication meets the minimum requirements of American National Standard for Information Sciences—Permanence of Paper for Printed Library Materials, ANSI/NISO Z39.48-1992.
Manufactured in the United States of America.

A special thank you to my husband, Jeffrey; my children: James, Jared, and ElizabethAnne; my dad, Ed; and to Joan, my best friend and mom, who titled the book and has always encouraged and supported me. Each of you has played a special role in my life, now reflected in my writing. I love you!

Contents

Acknowledgments		vii
Introduction		ix
1	What New Teachers Need to Know	1
2	The School Year	17
3	Professional Aspects	25
4	Connecting the Classroom to the Real World	39
Appendix A: Internet Resources		69
Appendix B: Parent–Teacher Communication		85
About the Author		97

Acknowledgments

This handbook was developed specifically for the first-year teacher or new building transfer. The idea and format for this project is based on a handbook I received as a new teacher from the Wisconsin Education Association Council's (WEAC) Instruction and Professional Development Committee (IPD): *The Beginning Teacher Handbook: A Book of Firsts* (1989). After teaching for ten years, I went into school administration and still found myself referring back to the handbook as I worked with my own faculty. I began to add, delete, and modify based on the needs of my faculty and the specific building in which I served. As I began working with student teachers, candidates for alternative licensure, and students in upper-level coursework through CESA and local universities, I identified three main areas that were challenging to new teachers: time management, classroom management, and lesson planning. The document before you is a culmination of

WEAC's beginning teacher handbook, additional resources, and years of experience in working with new and pre-service teachers to pinpoint areas that are challenging and to provide assistance or resources before the challenges became problematic. It has been cross-referenced with information from teachers new to the field between 2000 and 2004, with the assistance of Dr. William Henk (dean of Marquette University's School of Education) and Dr. James Juergensen (dean of Concordia University of Wisconsin's School of Education). Thank you to the educators who took the time to candidly answer questions and thoughtfully reflect upon their new placement in the field. The information shared will enhance the art and science of teaching, make the transition to teaching (or teaching in a new building) easier, and provide a successful experience for teachers, their colleagues, and the children whose lives they touch.

Introduction

Welcome! You have joined a dynamic, dedicated group of professionals. As you read through this book, many questions will arise. Feel free to bring these questions to your principal, your assigned mentor, or any staff member—since educators recognize the importance of and operate as a team. Your challenge is to engage your students while teaching the assigned curriculum and to assist each student in reaching his or her potential. In the words of Sidney Hook, "Everyone who remembers his own educational experience remembers teachers, not methods and techniques." Now the opportunity to help shape the future lies within you.

Cura personalis: care for the person. Let no one fall between the cracks.

Chapter One

What New Teachers Need to Know

OVERVIEW OF THE SCHOOL

Every school has a culture of its own, even if it's part of a larger district. It's important to gain an understanding of the school and the district in which you'll work, as well as your role as an educator within that district. To better understand your district, you should find out:

- The school district or central governing agency of your school, the policymakers, hiring agent/s, and overall chain of command. Get to know them by name and position, and gain an understanding of district protocol.
- The people who prepare, present, and report on the budget, and those who determine budget cuts.
- Area economics.

- New developments and subdivisions in your district.
- Demographics of your school.
- Current enrollment and recent trends.
- Feeder schools.
- Educational and extracurricular programs within your school.
- Your school's open enrollment plan, if any.
- The number of faculty members, support staff, and administrators.
- Points of interest about the school.
- Specific instructional methods used district- or schoolwide.
- Areas of recognition for the school, personnel, or students.
- Areas identified for improvement within the school.
- Parental involvement within the school.
- Schoolwide activities that parents and students anticipate.
- Issues that currently face this particular school and this particular district, and the plan (both short- and long-term) to handle them. How will your role as an educator fit in to this plan?

WHY HAVE A HANDBOOK?

Your initial year of teaching will be filled with transition: a new building, a new boss, new colleagues, new students and families, new rules, a new schedule and curriculum, and possibly even a new community.

The change from student to teacher can be simultaneously exciting and exhausting. It's said that it takes a person three years to learn a job and become familiar with both the available resources and required procedures. As reported by Heller in *Teachers Wanted: Attracting and Retaining Good Teachers*:

> A study published in the *American Educational Research Journal* and conducted by Richard M. Ingersoll, an associate professor of education and sociology at Philadelphia University, found the average yearly turnover rate in education is 13.2 percent as compared to 11 percent in other professions. Even more significant to the problem under discussion here is that 29 percent of new teachers leave education within their first three years, and by the end of five years, 39 percent have left (Viadero, 2002, p. 7). Ingersoll concludes that educators should spend less time on recruitment efforts and put more effort into retaining the teachers they have. . . . To make matters worse, the teachers who leave tend to be the best new recruits (Gordon and Maxey, 2000, p. 8). (p. 4–5)

The frustration that results from inexperience, isolation, and the lack of practical know-how can be overwhelming to the beginner. Keep in mind that your colleagues had to start somewhere; every one of them had a first year of teaching and most will have tales to tell. Teaching is virtually the only profession where a beginner is fully responsible for all aspects of his or her profession from the first day and, in fact, is expected to perform the same tasks as an experienced professional. True "on the job" training.

Many times teachers feel isolated, but there's no reason for that isolation. Early in your professional career, try to develop the perspective that teaching is a cooperative and collaborative undertaking. Be willing to ask questions and exchange ideas with your colleagues. Beginning teachers are often assigned a mentor teacher during their first year. This person is an experienced and effective teacher who communicates well and is willing to share knowledge and insights into the profession with you. This book is to be used in conjunction with your professional colleague. It will assist in asking questions, finding answers, and generating discussion.

Your initial year of teaching presents many "firsts." For the first time you'll be on your own in a classroom. For the first time you might be asked to teach a student whose native language isn't English, assign detention, or handle a fight on the playground. For the first time you might find yourself in a room of 28 students, nine of whom have special needs, with no aide assigned to you. This book has been designed to help you begin to anticipate some of these firsts. Having the opportunity to think about or talk about some common situations before you actually encounter them can assist you when you actually have to handle that situation. In the words of Franklin Roosevelt, "Make the mistakes of yesterday your lessons for today."

BEFORE THE FIRST DAY OF SCHOOL

It isn't uncommon for educators to begin working long before that exciting first day of school when the children arrive. How you prepare for that first day can make a big difference in your success. Since the first day sets the tone for your new school year, your approach and preparation will make a difference in how that first day, week, month, quarter, semester, and year of school will go for you in your new teaching position. A little time invested in advance will be beneficial in the long run.

Part of good teaching is finding the time to think about the things you do as a teacher. To help develop the habit of reflection, keep a daily journal where you can record the day's experiences; your thoughts on what went on in your classroom; and the questions, concerns, and ideas for teaching that you have each day. You'll be truly amazed at the growth you see in yourself when you reread the journal later. Another easy way to document your reflective teaching is within your lesson plans. Good teachers can usually identify what went well and what didn't go so well within a lesson. Documenting these observations within the plan will assist you when teaching that lesson, unit, or chapter in the future. This holds true with teacher-prepared as well as published materials. For example, if your students were totally confused by directions on a worksheet, are you going to continue to use that worksheet as written, or can you make adjustments in your teaching, the directions on the worksheet, or the assignment to make the worksheet less confusing? Better yet, question yourself: Does a worksheet reflect the best method of assessment, or is there an alternative assessment you could use to avoid the confusion?

Each and every school is unique. Therefore, not all ideas listed here will apply to you and your new teaching position. Find out as much as you can about your school. Call the school and ask when you can stop in. Make note of the telephone number, facsimile number, and address of your school, then visit. While you're there, be sure to find:

- A map of the school showing fire exits and extinguishers, which should be posted in each classroom and visible to students.
- The main office.
- The principal's office.
- Your classroom.
- The library/learning resource center.
- Where audio-visual equipment and materials are housed as well as check out or sign-up procedures.
- The healthroom.
- Other rooms, such as the gymnasium or computer lab.
- Where your mailbox is located.
- The teachers' lounge, faculty lunchroom, and faculty workroom.

- The faculty restroom.
- The faculty parking lot, student parking lot, and where to obtain a parking permit if necessary.
- A school calendar.
- Computers and software.
- Copy equipment, toner, and paper.
- Location of general supplies, the person to go to when supplies are low, and the procedure for ordering.
- Secretarial assistance.
- Student health information (allergies, seizures, diabetes, etc.).
- Lunchroom and meal purchase procedures for students. Are off-campus lunches allowed?
- Location of maintenance office. Get to know maintenance personnel by name and work shifts.
- Location and use of work orders.
- Schedules of colleagues within your department.
- Know state and local requirements for your content area.
- Procedures for locking down the school and where guests sign in. Does the school use visitor badges?
- Alarm/security information. Find out if hanging items from blinds or ceiling tiles will set off your security system, if cameras or codes are used, and what you need to know about them.
- Location and use of faculty forms.
- Location of the laminator and fax machines.
- What you need to know about the telephone system. Are there different rings? Are teachers expected to

answer the telephone if office personnel are not able to do so? How do you transfer calls?
- Use of the public announcement or intercom system.

BE SURE TO FIND OUT

Prior to the start of the school year, get to know the professional expectations of your position. This will alleviate questions or tension in the future. Here are some recommendations:

- Obtain a copy of your contract. Know the terms and renewal process.
- Is there a probationary period in your contract?
- What are the requirements for tenure?
- Obtain copies of the faculty and family handbooks.
- Know what benefits you are entitled to, and be sure to complete all necessary paperwork to participate in these benefits.
- Obtain a copy of the pay scale and pay schedule.
- Find out about various types of time off, such as sick, personal, professional, vacation, funeral, and jury duty. How to call these days in and to whom?
- What deductions (e.g., Social Security, insurance, and flex benefits) are taken from your pay?
- Learn about the retirement plan and how it works.
- Fill out necessary forms the school requires to be included in your personnel file: application, resume, philosophy of teaching, transcripts, I-9, criminal

background check (national check and fingerprints), contract, attendance, observations/evaluations, W2, insurance enrollment, flexible spending account enrollment, teaching license (or certification plan), physical examination (including drug test and TB test), and improvement plan (if necessary).
- Is there a teachers' union? How does the union work? Is membership required? Who is the union representative for your building, district, or area? How has the union assisted teachers in the past? How are relations between the teachers, union, and district? What do you need to know? Have contracts been issued on time? Have the teachers walked out or participated in movements to show dissatisfaction? What are the union's expectations of you as a new teacher?
- Does the district contribute toward your continued education?
- Who do you contact if there is a problem with your paycheck or benefits?
- Are there opportunities for stipends?
- Are faculty committees established? For what purpose(s)? How often do they meet?
- What's the schedule and typical agenda for faculty/staff meetings?
- What are the contracted hours for teachers?
- What are the office hours of the school?
- Locate the curriculum for your assigned area.
- Check state standards and local benchmarks that you'll be responsible for in your new teaching placement.

- Where do you place outgoing mail?
- What is the homework policy?
- What's the school policy for students who miss work?
- Is homework given out early for vacations? Are report cards or progress reports issued early?
- What's the procedure for dealing with disciplinary problems?
- Make sure you know the school policy for referrals: special education, speech and language, gifted and talented, and Title I assistance.
- What's the policy on dispensing medication?
- What are the procedures for fire and tornado drills?
- What are the procedures for petty cash purchases?
- How is information communicated between the home and school, and between administration and staff?
- Make sure you have the forms you'll need the first week of school, and know what information should be included on each and how they are handled (e.g., in reporting student absences or tardiness or as hall passes).
- What should you do in the event of teacher illness (who to contact and when, lesson plans, and materials for your substitute)?
- What are the summer school opportunities?
- Who's responsible for cleaning the teachers' lounge, microwave, refrigerator, etc.?
- What should you do in case of an emergency (security, medical, CPR, crisis intervention team, etc.)?

- Know the location of and how to complete progress reports.
- Know how to have an announcement read over the PA system.
- Understand the use of passes in your building (e.g., for lockers, the restroom, the office, and the counselor).
- Sign up for the computer lab and media such as TV, VCR, or DVD.
- What supervisory duties are you responsible for (e.g., lunch duty, after-school duty, detention, in-school suspension, or hallways)?
- What are the expectations for homeroom and the morning routine, e.g., the pledge of allegiance and announcements?
- Are there special schedules to know about (e.g., shortened days for teacher in-service, focus groups or advisory periods)?
- What is the dismissal procedure for students?
- Where should you keep your lesson plans for easy access by a substitute teacher? Are you required to turn in a copy? If so, to whom and when?
- What are the school grading policies for scale and honor roll?
- What kind of celebrations (holidays, birthdays, and other events) does the school have?
- How are deliveries to students, such as flowers or balloons, handled?
- Are there spirit days?
- What are the assignment of lockers, cubbies, or other spaces to place personal items?

- How is the distribution of information to parents handled (office to parent or teacher to parent)?
- Inquire about which events are important to the school and the parents. That doesn't mean you *have* to do it, but be cognizant of what's important to the school community and decide if the event fits into the curriculum.
- Which extracurricular activity will you coordinate and supervise? Plan early.
- Is there a master calendar on which to place events such as assemblies, field trips, and extracurricular activities?

BE SURE TO MEET

- Your colleagues. They are excellent resources, open and helpful. Meet your department chairperson. See if staff members socialize outside of the school setting and participate if possible.
- Your mentor. Make a list of questions you might need to ask this key person. Don't be hesitant to ask about things that are of concern to you. It's a good idea to ask your mentor about in-service opportunities and to assist you for the beginning of school. Work with your mentor to develop what will probably be your first professional collaboration.
- The principal, the educational leader of the school. Discuss his or her vision for the school and its atmosphere or school climate.
- Assistant principal(s). In many cases the assistant principal is responsible for discipline and scheduling.

- The secretary, the principal's right-hand person. This person is often the key to the everyday running of the school and is knowledgeable about finances, procedure, policy, supply orders, book orders, materials, and buses. The secretary is a great resource.
- Maintenance personnel. Get to know them by name and by shift. Use work orders as necessary. Find out the cleaning schedule, e.g., are classrooms cleaned every day? How often are the floors mopped? Who's responsible for wiping desktops and how often is this done? How is recycling handled?
- Support personnel, e.g., school nurse or educational assistants.
- Parent volunteers. What's the level of parental involvement and in what capacity do parents volunteer?
- School board members. Find out about elections, roles, members, subcommittees, and length of terms.
- PTA members. Find out about elections, duties, subcommittees, members, involvement in school functions, primary functions, special events, fundraising participation, etc.

BE SURE TO HAVE

- Your schedule.
- Lesson plans with duties noted.
- Curriculum guides for your assigned content area or special area.
- State standards and local benchmarks you're responsible for in your assigned placement.

- Adequate numbers of copies of the textbooks you're using.
- Family, faculty, and new teacher handbooks.
- Collective bargaining agreement.
- Keys and security information.
- Class lists.
- Locker assignments.
- Attendance forms and procedure.
- Supplies ordered for your classroom: grade book or computer codes, lesson plan book, paper, pencils, pens, paper clips, rubber bands, masking tape, scotch tape, scissors, chalk, dry erase markers, stapler, and staples.
- Classroom budget and procedures for purchasing items for your classroom.
- Staff telephone numbers via emergency tree or faculty directory.
- Information from the principal.
- Completed personnel file.
- Information and procedures on continuing education credits.
- A staff member to eyeball notes home to the parents. An extra set of eyes can be very helpful.

BE SURE YOU KNOW

Decide what you'll teach and do the first day of school. Make a detailed schedule for the first day. Be sure to include the times for each class, your lunch, assigned duties, administrative paperwork, and a breather for yourself.

Write down everything, including what you plan to cover, procedures, and at what point you plan to do various activities. Plan at least twice as much as you think you'll have time to cover in a day. Plan several extra activities in case some or all of your students quickly complete scheduled activities. Try to give work that all students can complete successfully and that you can correct and return the next day.

Know the curriculum and scope and sequence chart, and think about how you're going to teach the material. Review all lesson plans. Be sure to have materials prepared and copied in advance. You should also:

- Straighten your room and try to make it look inviting.
- Decorate the bulletin boards. All boards need to be covered. The board should change with seasons and events, with the exception of the calendar. Keep it simple and tasteful but unusual and exciting.
- Arrange the desks and chairs, making sure that all desks have a clear visual path to the board, overhead, or other necessary areas of the classroom. Check the classroom information to see if preferential seating is necessary for any students.
- Copy, collect, and organize your materials. Be prepared: students know if you're organized and prepared or not. Don't wait until the morning of or class period before doing any necessary copying.

Machinery isn't always dependable, particularly in humid weather.
- Familiarize yourself with attendance and pass procedures.
- Think about the climate of your classroom, which will evolve as a direct result of your decisions as a teacher. Classroom rules of conduct should be clear and posted. It's much easier to loosen up as you go along than to try to tighten up after your students have already been given too much freedom. Be cognizant of teacher talk vs. student talk. Decide what you'll share about yourself with your students. Decide on the degree of formality in your teaching style.
- Know where forms are located.
- Demonstrate professionalism, including your attire (no midriff shirts, miniskirts, flip-flops, etc.). Learn about your district and building guidelines regarding professional attire.
- Can teachers consume beverages while they teach (e.g., coffee, tea, or water)? What about food and snacks?
- Can students consume beverages or snacks in the classroom?
- Where are vending machines located and what are the rules for when students can use them?

Chapter Two

The School Year

AS THE SCHOOL YEAR APPROACHES

If you plan to drive to school each morning, drive it once during the time you would normally commute to school to find the best route and check traffic patterns and time. Place yourself on a "school training schedule" to get used to the hours. Subscribe to a local newspaper, or view it online. Become familiar with local attitudes, ideas and community values. Enjoy a short vacation, if possible. Complete or reschedule projects to alleviate stress once the school year begins. Get a large calendar for your desk and jot down important dates, upcoming events and commitments, and appointments. Get to know your community:

- Emergency telephone numbers
- Post office locations and zip codes
- Utility companies that serve you

- Recreation, exercise, and sports activities that are nearby
- Public library and Bookmobile
- Parks, zoos, museums, theatres, historical sites, etc.
- Local universities and colleges
- Radio and television stations
- Grocery stores, bookstores, shopping malls, and education supply stores
- Banking institutions: locations, telephone numbers, and hours
- Medical facilities
- Local parking regulations (snow dates, alternate parking, etc.)
- Dates for special events at the school (open house, concerts, talent show, theatrical productions, etc.)

Check into collaborative efforts and partnerships between the school and local universities or businesses. For example, many local universities offer scholarships or reciprocal relationships to teachers. Some schools work with area businesses to upgrade computer equipment, and then donate used equipment to organizations.

THE FIRST DAY

As you actually begin the practice of teaching, you might find the following suggestions helpful:

- Greet students as they enter the building.
- Assign seats or allow students to choose. Either way, make a seating chart so you can call on students by name during the period.
- Set expectations with students for students.
- Review the specific rules for behavior along with their consequences and rewards, and do so in a non-threatening way. Be firm but fair. Maintain discipline. It's recommended to post no more than five classroom rules.
- If you give a homework assignment the first night, make it one that your students can complete successfully and that you can correct and return the next day.
- Check your mailbox every day, several times if possible. Messages are left throughout the day. The intercom system or telephones should be used only when deemed necessary in order to minimize classroom disruptions.
- Use pencil the first week or two, as changes are common.
- Plan to arrive at school early and stay late for at least the first few weeks. Teaching during this period is likely to be tiring, so keep your personal commitments to a minimum. Be prepared to be tired for a few weeks.
- Clarify your homework policy.
- Realize that there will be many forms and much paperwork to do. Don't let it overwhelm you.

- Have a list of supplies you want your students to purchase. These are typically distributed to families in the spring and then again in the fall.
- Recognize that you don't know everything and that you don't *need* to know everything. Be willing to ask questions and eager to collaborate with your colleagues.

THE FIRST WEEK

- Get to know your colleagues. Get in the habit of exchanging ideas and professional insights.
- Get to know the special education resources and referral process.
- Get to know resources available, including library, computer, etc.
- Identify student health problems. Note any possible hearing or vision problems for preferential seating and parental contact. Decide what to do in case of a medical emergency.
- Familiarize yourself with procedures for student tardiness or truancy.
- Familiarize yourself with local procedures for student abuse or neglect.
- Locate telephones that are accessible to teachers. Check local policies on cell phones for both teachers and students.
- Know who's in charge when the principal is out of the building.

- Keep accurate records of attendance, behavior, assignments, and fee collection.
- Prepare a substitute folder.
- Learn students' names as quickly as possible. They appreciate it, and they'll respond better when addressed by name.
- Keep a professional journal. Record daily questions, thoughts, and impressions about your teaching. Consider what worked, what didn't work, and why. Consider what sort of student responses occurred in class. Consider which students were successful that day, which weren't, and possible reasons. Review and reflection are the first steps in individual professional growth and development. When reading your journal, you'll recognize the journey you've endured, see your growth, and have something tangible to turn back to when entering year two.

THE FIRST MONTH

- Know when regular meetings are planned (e.g., for staff, school board, and PTA).
- Know the policy and procedure for scheduling field trips, collecting money, and ordering transportation.
- Know the location of student files.
- Know the procedure and dates for sending out student progress reports.
- Know the procedures for assemblies.

- Find out your school's policy on attending teachers' conventions. Is it a contracted day? Is attendance mandatory or optional?
- Get to know the overall makeup of the student body.
- Get to know your colleagues. Make an effort to do things with other teachers.
- Get involved in school activities.
- It's usually about this time that the daily needs of the teaching profession begin to overwhelm the beginning teacher, corresponding with a decline in enthusiasm and fading of idealism. Be cognizant of this and don't let it happen. Your enthusiasm for students and your idealism about what teachers can do is vital. Preserve them! Remember that you aren't alone. Discuss your feelings with colleagues. Collaborate, communicate, and cooperate with them to accomplish your common goal of providing a quality education for the students and assisting all students in reaching their potential.

THE FIRST QUARTER

- Get to know the various student organizations, clubs, and teams.
- Attend a school activity voluntarily. This can mean a great deal to parents and students alike.
- Know the procedure for identifying students who need assistance and referring them for special education.

- Know the resources for gifted and talented students.
- Become familiar with other special programs unique to your school, and contact the people associated with them.
- Find out where to obtain information on school closings and what obligations you have.
- Learn how to fill out report cards and where to document state standards and local benchmarks.
- Familiarize yourself with policies on grading, detentions, suspensions, and graduation requirements.
- Learn how to figure and submit honor roll lists. Look into honors programs for students, e.g., presidential scholar.

THE FIRST SEMESTER

- Get to know budgeting procedures.
- Know the procedure for determining need, placing, and recording an order.
- Get to know procedures for using media in the classroom. Can you sign up for library or computer use outside of specialist class time? How do you sign up for a television, VCR, DVD, or projector? What ratings are acceptable within your school? Do you need parental permission for media? What media are available, e.g., filmstrips and movies? Are other resources available, such as a local public library or another school district? What's your reason for choosing media? How will the media effectively tie

in to your curriculum? Will it enhance classroom discussion before and/or after a lesson? Will it inspire student writing or intrigue students to learn more about the topic? Will you use it to compare a novel to a movie? Do you need to show the whole video or just a segment to get your point across? Did you preview the video to ensure it's at the appropriate age or grade level? Did you test the equipment to be sure it works? Is there a glare on the screen? Is the quality of the tape okay? How is the volume? How will you promote active participation, e.g., study guides, questions, note taking, problem solving, alternative endings, or letters to an author or film director?
- Get to know free material resources.

Chapter Three

Professional Aspects

SETTING GOALS

It's imperative for teachers to set goals. Goal setting allows them to improve the quality of their teaching. Although the process might seem complex and demanding, it's necessary in order to create excellence in education.

Goals are directly tied to the teaching standards that identify benchmarks of effective teaching. The wording of the goals should reflect the "knowledge, skills, and dispositions" (KSD) tied to the teaching standards. By using the KSD as a guide, pre-service teachers can gain an understanding of these standards and what they need to attain as a teacher, while new teachers have documentation readily available to them to keep in mind their direction, goals, continual assessment, and reflective practice.

Through the process of setting goals, individual teachers take into account the community in which they teach, the culture of the school, and the individuality of the students, and adapt their knowledge of teaching to ensure effective student learning.

The goals that are chosen need to be measurable. Teachers must determine the type of evaluation and assessment they believe will best demonstrate improvement. With student teachers, evaluation and assessment that demonstrates attainment of goals is the case more often than not.

You must move beyond collection of data to understand effective teaching and student learning, and meeting the needs of students. Reflect on where you are as an educator, and set your goals based on the next steps of where you want to or need to be.

Goals reflect both long- and short-range plans for professional growth and development. Although the enhancement of teaching skills is recognized as a life long process, goals define the planned areas of focus for a predetermined timeline. For example, if a student teacher is in a tri-placement due for early childhood licensure, the goals would be specific to each of the three individual placements. As a new teacher entering the field of education, your goals might break down by quarter, semester or school year.

The number of goals should be a workable number, and as written they should be attainable within the timeframe. Be careful to challenge yourself without frustrating or setting yourself up for failure.

Seek guidance and support to achieve success in reaching or even surpassing your goals.

MAINTAINING PROFESSIONALISM

Teaching is a profession. Other professionals in the field, as well as those outside the field such as parents or lawmakers, have certain expectations of teachers. People often believe that earning a degree means they've earned professional status, but being a professional goes beyond earning a degree. While there are several meanings of the word, *professionalism* in the context I'm using refers to having the qualifications of a particular profession and being well-trained, good at what you do, and dependable. Therefore, merely doing a job for a certain number of years doesn't make you a professional, nor does having acquired a particular degree. Certain characteristics are necessary for professionalism. These include:

- Being a role model: character, integrity, honesty, forthrightness, trustworthiness
- Being a reflective practitioner and striving for continual improvement
- Being responsible and accountable
- Projecting a professional image, including attire and appropriate language
- Displaying professional maturity and conduct
- Maintaining confidences and confidentiality

- Being willing to take direction and follow instruction
- Accepting your current place in a system and following protocol or chain of command in working within that system
- Addressing others by title
- Being a team player
- Demonstrating respect toward students, parents, school board members, administrators, etc.
- Being loyal to your organization and co-workers, e.g., honoring and not abusing contractual issues
- Doing what's right
- Planning
- Making decisions
- Communicating openly and appropriately
- Pressing for excellence
- Doing your job to the best of your ability, without constant direction and without excuses

Remember that your students and school families see you in the community, such as at the grocery store or a local restaurant, as well as in the school setting. You've chosen a career in which you're a public servant. As such, you live your life in a fishbowl for all to see, and your personal life will be public.

LEGAL ISSUES

From calling grades aloud in class to searching lockers, the education system has come under fire and been challenged through the legal system. Many unions and districts offer legal services to a member or an employee. Ask about your legal benefits.

Following is a list of some policies you will want to check into prior to the students' attendance. Though not a comprehensive list, it will give you an idea of some issues you might face as an educator:

- Due process
- Prior notice of expectations
- Notification of applied penalty
- Notification of charges against a student
- Allowing student to respond
- Providing a hearing to ensure a fair decision
- Providing equal opportunities for students regardless of race, religion, sexual orientation, gender, socioeconomic status, handicap/s, behavior, etc.
- Choice of classroom management strategies
  - Corporal punishment
  - Time out
  - Detentions and suspensions
  - Homework policies
  - Dress codes and uniforms
  - Participation in and suspension from extracurricular activities
  - Participation in and suspension from field trips
  - Search and seizure (e.g., lockers, cars, backpacks, or purses)
  - Fights
  - Language, threats, and bullying

- Weapons
- "No tolerance" policies

A TIME FOR REFLECTION

Reflective teaching goes hand-in-hand with the effective planning and execution of lessons. Unfortunately, a high number of demands require prioritizing within limited time allotments, and these demands often outweigh the reflection on past practice. Yet it's important for teachers—all teachers—to realize the importance of reflection, for it's open and honest reflection that allows us to identify our successes, failures, strengths, weaknesses, and changes we can make. Good teachers will tell you that they've had lessons that didn't go as planned. Some teachers will even find humor in lessons that "bombed." Reflection and change are components of good teaching.

The following questions are designed to help you focus your thinking on past professional practice. They're designed to develop the habit of professional thoughtfulness and personal evaluation, and to stimulate a search for more effective teaching practices. You can use your responses to these questions as journal entries or to stimulate collaborative discussion with your mentor or other colleagues:

- What kinds of questions have you been asking during classroom discussions or on your exams? Do

those questions stimulate thinking and creativity as well as recall? Do some of your questions have a variety of appropriate answers?
- What is the rate of student success in your classroom? Of student failure? What kinds of students tend to succeed? To fail? Is there a pattern?
- Do you think students enjoy coming to your classroom to learn? What are the conditions that appear to contribute to the atmosphere of joyful learning? How can those conditions be enhanced in your classroom?
- What is your relationship with the parents of your students? Have you developed any mutual problem-solving relationships? How many parents have you contacted with a "good news" message?
- Do you have a professional "best friend"? Have you invited that colleague to watch you teach? Have you watched your colleague teach? Do you have time committed to a discussion of professional matters?
- Do students leave your classroom open to future learning?
- What professional journal are you now reading regularly? What is its appeal?
- How do you respond to the range of student abilities in your classroom? Do you ask students to learn alone? To help each other learn? What lessons have you planned to facilitate cooperative learning?
- How do you think about the content you teach? Is it something external that students must absorb? Are meanings "out there" waiting to be internalized? Or

do students create meaning in your classroom? When do they do that?
- Most learning is hard work and requires student engagement to occur at an optimal level. Engagement can be inferred from the time students are willing to spend on academic tasks, the intensity of their concentration, their enthusiasm, and the care they take in completing their tasks. Are your students engaged?

Following are some prompts for your professional journal:

- As the school year begins, I'm most nervous or anxious about . . .
- As the school year begins, I'm most excited about . . .
- I encouraged my students to think critically when . . .
- I encouraged by students to problem-solve when . . .
- I engaged my students in the lesson by . . .
- I saw how excited my students were when . . .
- I could improve that lesson by . . .
- I need to contact . . .
- My most challenging student . . .
- Something I learned from my students is . . .
- I wish my students would . . .
- I wish my district would . . .
- I can affect my students' lives by . . .
- My students affect my life by . . .
- My favorite lesson this week was . . .
- My students really enjoyed . . .

- I felt overwhelmed when . . .
- I remembered to praise my students when . . .
- My most creative lesson has been . . .
- What I need to focus on is . . .
- I know my students are learning because . . .
- Some great questions my students have asked are . . .
- I felt uncomfortable when . . .
- I am glad I went into teaching because . . .

INDUCTION ACTIVITIES

Unanticipated events will occur. Be flexible and adaptable in responding to the unexpected. Ask your mentor for suggestions on how to deal with situations such as:

- A child becoming ill
- A student who has a health concern, e.g., diabetes, asthma, or allergies
- A student becoming emotional in class
- Dealing with death (relative, friend, or pet)
- A student sharing sensitive information with you regarding substance abuse, sexual abuse, pregnancy, etc.
- A parent who is angry or unreasonable
- A student refusing to do what you asked of him or her
- A student falling asleep in class
- Students refusing to participate in your planned activity

- Being called into the office during a class
- Non-English-speaking students being assigned to your class
- Saying or doing something embarrassing in front of the class
- A fight breaking out and you being the nearest faculty member
- Suspecting substance abuse by a student or colleague

In addition to questions such as these, it's strongly recommended that the beginning teacher have regularly planned discussions with his or her mentor. Collaboration and professional discussion are key to professional growth and development. Topics of discussion could include (items followed by an asterisk are addressed in more detail in chapter 1):

1. Classroom management*
    - Heading off inappropriate behavior*
    - Classroom rules*
    - Student behavior
    - Listening
    - Student motivation
    - Reward systems for students
    - Policies for planned absence and make-up work
2. Time management*
    - Overall planning
    - Specific lessons and transition periods
    - Balancing personal and professional duties with-

out becoming overwhelmed
3. Planning effective lessons*
   - Components of an effective lesson*
4. Instructional strategies*
   - Choosing the best instructional strategy for that lesson, objective, or assessment with that particular group of students*
   - Discipline procedures
   - Detention (when is it held, what do they do, how long is it?)
   - Uniform or dress code (what to do when a student shows up out of uniform or dress code, consequences, warm weather dress)
   - Bullying
   - Addressing the situation
   - Not turning a deaf ear
   - Identifying the students at fault and the consequence earned
   - Deciding if the parent(s) or principal need to be notified
5. Evaluating student performance
   - Consistent with school grading scale
   - Record keeping
   - Filling out a report card or progress report
   - Parent–teacher–student conferences*
   - Different forms of evaluation
   - Parent–teacher communication*
6. Multicultural awareness
   - Bilingual/bicultural resources
   - Appropriate teaching techniques to help the child

- Language abilities: monolingual/bilingual, language spoken in the home
- Cultural diversity
7. Teaching styles
    - Development of your own teaching style*
    - Professional classroom demeanor*
    - Classroom strategies
    - Developing communication skills
    - Using community resources
    - Learning styles: both yours and the students'
    - Teaching techniques, e.g., cooperative learning and differentiated instruction
8. Supervision and evaluation
    - Clinical and standards-based supervision
    - Being observed and supervised: new teachers are observed four times throughout the year and veteran teachers are observed only once
    - Confidentiality and evaluation
    - Expectations for the beginning teacher
10. Professional growth and development opportunities
    - Professional organizations in your discipline or area of special interest
    - Investigate upcoming conferences, workshops, and the policy that pertains to your attendance at them
11. Special education
    - Names of students
    - Resources
    - Instructional strategies

- Appropriate materials
- Modification
- Use of the learning resource center (LRC)
12. Technology in the classroom
    - Acceptable use policy (AUP)
    - Technology integration such as VHS, DVD, CDs, Internet searches, bookmarking sites, Power Point presentations, and political cartoons
    - Inappropriate use has consequences: be in tune with the sites your students are visiting and games they're playing
    - Virus protection
    - E-mail use by students
    - E-mail use by faculty

Chapter Four

Connecting the Classroom to the Real World

If you're wondering what's in store for you, you're in good company. The experiences of first-year teachers run the gamut, from those who have a wonderful experience to those who cry on a daily basis. Hopefully, experienced teachers will take new teachers under their wing and guide them in becoming excellent educators. This book cannot comprehensively answer every question or address every concern of a new teacher. So you can better understand some of the challenges you might face, this chapter provides the answers to a survey that was conducted with approximately 200 teachers (with an approximate 25% return rate) new to the field in 2000–2004. The survey asked the new teachers about topics such as difficulties they encountered in the school their first day, what information they needed as a new teacher, and what they considered to be the most important thing to know going into the job.

Chapter Four

QUESTIONS FOR A NEW HIGH SCHOOL TEACHER

- How do I handle discipline?
- Who do I see for what?
- How do I set the tone and establish authority?
- How do I motivate students?
- How do I motivate co-workers?
- What are the students supposed to know?
- Where is the curriculum located?
- What do the students already know?
- What resources do I have: people, books, Internet sites, etc.?
- How do I balance paperwork and teaching?
- What is the school climate like?
- How do I handle grading?
- How do I handle the parents or student fighting the grade earned?
- How do I handle a student who's absent or tardy all the time?
- What are the expectations placed upon me?
- What am I supposed to do?
- How do I plan lessons and learn time management?
- How do I handle different sections of the same class moving through the same material at a different rate?
- How is late work handled?
- How do report cards work?
- How do I participate in continuing education?
- How do I renew my license?
- What is the philosophy of the administration?
- Is there any parent involvement?

Connecting the Classroom to the Real World

- What are the politics within the school like?
- Is a map and tour of the building available for new staff?
- Where do I go to get materials and supplies?
- Who can I turn to for support?
- Will I keep my position or be displaced?
- Does the district appreciate me?
- Can I do this for the next 35 years?
- How do I find practical information, such as the location of the copy machine, when staff meetings are held, and how to issue student passes?
- Do we use a block schedule? Who's in charge of scheduling?
- How do I run the day-to-day classroom?
- How do I improve something at the school or district level without alienating myself from my colleagues and the administration?
- What are the procedures of the school?
- How do I teach students who are only four years younger than I am?
- How can I get the students to be patient with me as a new teacher?
- How are writing tests and assessments handled?
- Where's the handbook? Is it adhered to? Is there follow-through?
- How do I become more organized?
- How do I access materials before the start of school?
- How do I handle a late hire?
- How do I handle student attitude toward my subject, particularly if it's required?
- Am I prepared to teach?

- How do I project that I'm the teacher and I'm in charge?
- How do I handle changes in scheduling, room, or facility?
- Can I be myself?
- What benefits am I entitled to?
- How do I teach complex material at a high school level?
- What are my responsibilities to the district, school, and students?

WHAT NEW HIGH SCHOOL TEACHERS WANT

- Feedback from the principal and colleagues
- Strategies for classroom management
- Hands-on assessment tools
- Resources for at-risk or gray-area students
- Materials and supplies
- Curriculum
- Support
- A manual of "who's who" at the school and within the district
- One resource area to prepare a package for new staff with a parent handbook, staff directory, etc. so they don't have to be hunted down
- A calendar of events
- A tour of the school
- A detailed map of the school premises
- An orientation session for faculty new to the school

- A mentor
- To provide structure within the classroom
- To handle a large workload
- To reach the necessary standards by the end of the year

ADVICE FOR NEW HIGH SCHOOL TEACHERS

- Understand the politics you're dealing with.
- Get to know the policies you're responsible for enforcing.
- Set personal and professional goals.
- Use your colleagues.
- Know your material.
- Kids love attention and caring people.
- Listen!!
- Be confident.
- Focus on the good days.
- Get involved.
- The first days set the tone for the year.
- You're on your own.
- Keep a positive attitude and an open mind.
- Be flexible.
- Be prepared to make mistakes, and learn from them.
- Seek answers.
- Bring questions to your mentor.
- Have someone to provide support and give good advice.
- Put in extra time.
- Dress professionally.

- Use other teachers as a resource.
- Admit if you don't know something.
- Meet deadlines.
- Understand your students (background, history, needs).
- Don't be cliquey or align yourself with one group.
- Don't overextend yourself or volunteer for too many things.

QUESTIONS FOR NEW MIDDLE SCHOOL TEACHERS

- How do I set limits and stick to them?
- Am I teaching everything correctly?
- Are students learning?
- Why do I have so much work to do?
- What am I doing wrong?
- What are the school rules and regulations?
- When is my prep time?
- How many different classes do I have to prepare for?
- What do I do if some classes get ahead of other classes?
- What are the principal's expectations?
- What's the school community like?
- What types of students am I teaching?
- How do I track student achievement?
- What are the students' expectations?
- How do I maintain authority and respect at the same time?
- How do I make parental contact successful?

- Who makes copies?
- Are there discipline forms and what are the disciplinary procedures?
- Where do I get supplies and materials?
- Who helps with technology?
- What do I put in a substitute folder?
- What activities would benefit students most?
- Where do I go for support? Do I have a mentor? Do I use another teacher? My principal? The school office?
- Where do I go for support for the students? The counselor?
- How do I model classroom procedures?
- What are the routines and procedures of the school?
- How do I learn all of the students and their names?
- What's the curriculum for my content area? Is it used?
- What are the expectations of the faculty?
- What school policies do I need to know, e.g., dress code and recess?
- How do I keep smiling?
- Who's in charge of scheduling?
- How do I fill time?
- How will the students respond to me as a person?
- Who evaluates my lessons?
- How is classroom management and discipline addressed?
- What's the parent involvement?
- How do I draw the line between being a "friend" and being a "teacher"?
- Do I know my content area?
- Do I have the freedom to go beyond the curriculum?
- How are conferences handled?

- How are staff relations in the building? Are there conflicts?
- How do I set up my classroom?
- Who does the ordering?
- How are textbooks adopted, and how often?
- What's the grading scale? Do I need to do anything with honor roll?
- What duties do I have outside of teaching?
- What are my resources?
- How do I maintain respect?
- What's the process of participating in continuing education?
- Is there follow-through by the administration?
- How do you show the students that you're firm but compassionate?
- How do I compile teacher-made units?
- How do I stay organized?
- How do I avoid stress?
- How are emergencies handled?
- How do I get materials, such as teacher manuals, before the start of school?
- How do I plan my first year?
- How do I work with a diverse population?

WHAT NEW MIDDLE SCHOOL TEACHERS WANT

- Feedback from the principal and colleagues
- Strategies for classroom management
- Hands-on assessment tools

- Resources for at-risk or gray-area students
- Materials and supplies
- Curriculum
- Support
- A manual of "who's who" at the school and within the district
- Having one resource area prepare a package for new staff with a parent handbook, staff directory, etc. so they do not have to be hunted down
- A calendar of events
- A tour of the school
- A detailed map of the school premises
- An orientation session for faculty new to the school
- A mentor
- To provide structure within the classroom
- To handle a large workload
- To reach the necessary standards by the end of the year

ADVICE FOR NEW MIDDLE SCHOOL TEACHERS

- Understand the politics you're dealing with.
- Get to know the policies you're responsible for enforcing.
- Set personal and professional goals.
- Use your colleagues.
- Know your material.
- Kids love attention and caring people.
- Listen!!

- Be confident.
- Focus on the good days.
- Get involved.
- The first days set the tone for the year.
- You're on your own.
- Keep a positive attitude and an open mind.
- Be flexible.
- Be prepared to make mistakes, and learn from them.
- Seek answers.
- Bring questions to your mentor.
- Have someone to provide support and give good advice.
- Put in extra time.
- Dress professionally.
- Use other teachers as a resource.
- Admit if you don't know something.
- Meet deadlines.
- Understand your students (background, history, needs).
- Don't be cliquey or align yourself with one group.
- Don't overextend yourself or volunteer for too many things.

WHAT EVERY NEW TEACHER SHOULD KNOW

Develop Your Own Teaching Style

- Establish your own standards and expectations.
- Get students' attention before giving instructions. Learn their names quickly.

Connecting the Classroom to the Real World 49

- Get students on task.
- Give clear and specific directions.
- Set realistic timelines for tasks.
- Circulate among students while they're working, and make appropriate constructive comments.
- Adapt your teaching style to the level and type of student; it will differ with individual students and classes.
- Be flexible and continue to grow as a teacher.
- Try various approaches and reflect on what does and doesn't work. Consider why.
- Use questioning techniques; move toward more complex levels of questioning when student ability and maturity warrant.
- Avoid negativity in the teachers' lounge, parking lot, and athletic events.

Prepare Your Classroom

There's a lot of excitement and anticipation (and perhaps a little anxiety) when you finally have a classroom of your own. The preparations will most likely begin the summer prior to your fall teaching assignment. Here are some tips for your classroom:

- Cover all bulletin boards unless prohibited by fire codes. Use different materials, including butcher block paper, construction paper, fabric, newspaper, and wrapping paper. Most should change throughout the year, unless you have one board identified for

upcoming events, school news, or another heading that most likely won't change. But the information within the board still needs to be updated. Remember that bulletin boards should reflect the curriculum taught, and students love interactive bulletin boards. Students love to see their work in the spotlight, so try to have a piece from each student at some point in the quarter, semester, or year depending on the bulletin board.
- Avoid clutter. You might know where things are, but it can be distracting or overwhelming to students and doesn't present a very organized appearance to others entering your classroom.
- Check out your storage. Look at the closet, drawers, cupboards and other nooks and crannies available. Decide the best layout for your classroom, then organize from there. Plastic containers, baskets, stackable bins, nets, and cardboard storage units are useful items to store larger items. Smaller items can be kept in shoeboxes, kitchen cutlery trays, spice racks, ice cube trays, or plastic bowls with lids. Many types of magnetic products can attach to a chalkboard, desk, or other metal product. You might want to consider a pegboard with hanging hooks, holders, or even little drawers.
- Hang items from the ceiling. Mobiles and other projects are great to view hanging, where they can easily flow and move about. Hooks are often available, with some snapping over existing rails so as to be temporary. However, check with your building ad-

ministrator prior to hanging items due to security systems and fire codes.
- Be sure to locate normal office items such as scotch tape, paper clips, tissues, stapler (staples and staple remover), rubber bands, chalk, and dry erase markers.
- Do you need to reuse a poster, chart, or map that you wrote on for a lesson? To save your instructional materials, use a piece of laminate, clip it over the item, and use your erasable marker just as if it were on an overhead.
- Are you thinking of a classroom pet? Consider that taking care of a pet is quite a responsibility. Also consider the allergies and personal preferences of your students. For example, some students could be terrified of animals, while others might be very comfortable around them. Animals can teach many life lessons, increase vocabulary, or act as the center of a creative writing activity.

Create a Peaceful School Environment

To have a lasting effect on the school environment, an antiviolence campaign should demonstrate schoolwide commitment to training in and enforcing the campaign, build relationships between faculty and students as well as students, allow the students a voice in school decision-making, allow the students to express themselves without penalty or judgment, openly discuss safety procedures, work with community and family agencies, and emphasize prosocial behaviors such as sharing and helping.

Establish Routines

Routines are procedures that ensure effective use of time and space. Provide an explanation of the routine, and then practice it with the students. By dedicating a few hours at the beginning of the year to establishing and practicing routines, you'll avoid repetition and save time in the long run. Prior to the start of school, begin thinking about the who, what, when, where, and why of the classroom. Routines can be put in place for:

- Use of the restroom
- Getting necessary supplies from lockers, cubbies, or other parts of the classroom
- Group work
- Transitioning from one activity to another in the classroom
- Dismissal
- Entering the classroom
- Submission of homework
- Submission of late work
- Purchasing a lunch
- Cleaning up
- Acceptable use of a study hall
- Appropriately obtaining the teacher's attention
- Following procedure for academic instruction
- Keeping up with work for portfolios

- Use of special equipment, e.g., science labs, technology, or electronics

Head Off Inappropriate Behavior

- Call the student by name but don't disrupt a lesson to address the behavior. Wait and discuss the problem with the student privately.
- Use eye contact.
- Make sure to praise your students more quickly than criticizing them.
- Use cues such as the flick of an overhead light, a hand signal, body language, or a short verbal reprimand given at normal speaking tone. Raising one's voice is not a recommended approach of classroom management.
- Stand near the student to improve classroom control (use proximity).
- Tailor consequences to the specific individual and his or her specific action.
- Keep nonjudgmental anecdotal records on difficult students for selective use at conferences and for referrals. Record exactly what happened without interpretation.
- Keep your supervisor informed if a student is a problem. Don't be afraid to ask for help.
- Before contacting a parent about the student's inappropriate behavior, be sure you can discuss it calmly.
- Show your displeasure at a student's inappropriate behavior without implying that you dislike the student.

- Find something positive about each student and verbalize it.
- Don't threaten. Say what you mean, and mean what you say.
- Try to handle problems with students before sending them to the office. Reserve that option for major problems.
- Don't argue. Listen, summarize, describe the behavior and how it affects you and others, then give the student the opportunity to alleviate the problem.
- Offer self-instructions to students such as "*Think* of what you want to say, *raise* your hand, and *wait* to be called on."
- Openly communicate and collaborate with the student's parent or guardian.
- Remind students that every day offers a fresh start.

Plan Effective Lessons

Effective teachers keep students actively involved in their own learning. Engaging students leaves little time unaccounted for or wasted within a day, best using the limited amount of time with students. Some strategies to keep students engaged are:

- Have activities for the students to do when they enter the classroom or transition between content areas, for example, a journal entry, reflection, chapter summary, problem or puzzle of the day, definitions, or a few warm-up problems.

- Have materials organized and equipment set up prior to students' arrival.
- Involve all students at some point throughout the lesson.
- Offer a pace that's challenging but not frustrating.
- Prepare additional activities for students who complete work early.
- Determine how and when you'll help students requiring additional assistance.

Institute Instructional Strategies

When you choose your instructional strategy, you need to take into account the lesson's objective and assessment as well as the dynamics of that particular class. Some instructional strategies from which to choose are:

- Expository instruction such as lecture or textbook readings
- Direct instruction
- Mastery learning
- Computer-based instruction
- Online research
- Discovery learning
- In-class activities
- Computer simulators and applications
- Authentic activities
- Teacher questions
- Class discussion

- Reciprocal teaching
- Technology-based discussion
- Cooperative learning
- Peer tutoring
- Homework

MANAGE YOUR TIME WELL

Time management means balancing the different aspects of life. As an adult, you're used to making choices about how you spend your time. But take into consideration that your first three years of teaching, the first year in particular, might not be the smoothest. Planning takes additional time because you're most likely learning new curricula and using new textbooks. You're most likely going to spend many hours your first year writing up teacher resources like games, worksheets, rubrics and tests, then spending many more hours working out the kinks. In addition, you're learning a new position in a new school, with new faculty and staff, new students, new parents, and perhaps even in a new community. Give yourself a good three years to learn your position and become comfortable with your responsibilities.

Time management also includes accurately determining the amount of time lessons will take. New teachers often find they're short of material for their block of teaching time. If you don't know what to do with that time, the students are sure to fill it for you. Therefore, it's better to have too much material than not enough. As you work with the students, the curriculum, and your textbooks, you'll become more comfortable and gain better insight as to how much time the activities or projects will take.

Plan for the big picture first, then break the material into smaller units. As you work through your curriculum, your lessons should be tied to state standards (benchmarks or guidelines). Remember that you're responsible for your curriculum, and items like your textbook, computer, or pencil and paper are tools to assist you with instruction. As you become familiar with standardized tests you're responsible for administering within your content area or grade level, you might want to flip some of your units around to ensure that students receive instruction on specific concepts prior to being tested on them. I'm not saying to "teach to the test" but to merely be cognizant of your curriculum and when the students are tested on the material. For example, you might choose to teach a unit in October instead of March. The unit hasn't changed, but the students now have formal instruction in that area.

Always be certain to meet deadlines, whether for your department, school office, or district. Many times paperwork is necessary for state or federal reports. Be professional and provide the necessary information without requiring that someone chase you down or follow-up on paperwork.

Manage Your Classroom Effectively

Effective classroom management creates and maintains a classroom environment conducive to learning and achievement. Classroom management techniques *should* vary based on the instructional strategy the teacher is using. For example, when engaged in a hands-on activity, students have different expectations than when they're engaged in expository instruction.

As a teacher, you need to consider whether you want to have students actively participate in setting classroom rules (which provides ownership and a sense of community) or whether you want to establish rules on your own and explain them to the students. You also need to consider whether you want rules, or guidelines and classroom norms. Determine your approach in working with students when classroom rules are broken. Will outside factors and student diversity be taken into account, and if so, how? What's the best way to assist students in learning appropriate behavior? How do we teach children that mistakes are seldom fatal? How do we give students the tools they need to be accountable, learn, and grow from mistakes?

> To create and maintain a productive learning environment, effective teachers typically:
>
> - Physically arrange the classroom in a way that minimizes distractions and facilitates teacher–student interaction

- Create a climate in which students feel they belong and are intrinsically motivated to learn
- Set reasonable limits for behavior
- Plan activities that encourage on-task behavior
- Continually monitor what students are doing
- Modify instructional strategies when necessary. (Ormrod, 2006)

- Organize and prepare for each day's teaching. It shows that you enjoy teaching and take your responsibilities as a teacher seriously. Have a written plan to ensure that you've thought the lesson through and have all necessary materials and supplies. How can you expect your students to be prepared for class if you're making it up as you go along, or are scrambling for materials, supplies, or copies as the lesson begins? When you've completed the lesson, be a reflective practitioner and consider what went well as well as what you could have done differently with your lesson. Make notations or keep a journal, particularly your first year in the classroom.
- The classroom climate or psychological atmosphere we create must allow students to feel safe, secure, willing to make mistakes, and willing to take risks in an environment of mutual respect and support.
- To get students' attention, use cues such as eye contact, hand signals, and nonthreatening vocal contact.
- Avoid overstimulating students by presenting material and instructions in blocks, and offering only the materials necessary for the current lesson.

- Look over your curriculum at the beginning of the term to establish long-range goals. Be selective and adaptable based on class and student needs. Check and review your decision throughout the year. Make notations in your curriculum for that particular class that can be passed on to the next teacher.
- Assist students in taking responsibility by sharing upcoming events, projects, assignments, and deadlines. Establish a classroom routine that allows students to keep track of their work with little guidance. Allow students a choice in some assignments, such as providing a list of projects from which they can choose or establishing a due date with your assistance.
- Establish good rapport with students, parents, faculty, and staff. If you respect them, they'll respect you.
- Practice specific organizational skills with students. For example, make sure students write down their homework assignments in an assignment book and go over their tests carefully, not just looking at their grades, and verify that work goes home and isn't discarded.
- Give immediate and specific feedback if possible.
- Actively interact with every child every day. Humans are social by nature.
- You're responsible for the students in your classroom. Know what they're doing and become familiar with personality traits, which will give you insight into whether a student understands material or

not, is bored, is acting out or just having a bad day, etc.
- Establish a sense of community so every student feels that he or she belongs and is valued.
- Set reasonable limits on classroom behavior so students understand the expectations and are encouraged to continue to develop and grow. A few rules can be given by the teacher at the beginning of the year in an informative but not controlling manner. These rules should be reviewed often at first, occasionally throughout the year, and particularly after longer breaks so students are aware that the expectations haven't changed. Enforce the rules in a fair and consistent manner.
- Assist students in evaluating themselves: how they did, what they did right, what they did wrong, and what (specifically) they could do to change their behavior.
- Intervene promptly to stop inappropriate behavior.

Maintain a Professional Classroom Demeanor

- Model courtesy, politeness, and mutual respect.
- Use a "quiet" voice in the classroom.
- Be aware that your voice, movements, body language, and attire will be reflected in students' behavior.
- Dress professionally. Think about the image you're portraying.
- Be fair and consistent.

Set Classroom Rules

- They should be consistent with building policies.
- Make them with the cooperation of the students.
- Make them specific.
- See that they're clearly stated.
- Make them reasonable.
- Be sure they're enforceable.
- They should be logically consistent.
- Provide follow-through.
- Post expectations.
- Keep the list brief; too many "little" rules can be confusing.

Keep in Contact with Parents

- Decide what method of contact is best for the particular situation: personal conference, telephone, mail, note, or e-mail. Inquire as to whether the parent can receive telephone calls at work and the contact method he or she prefers.
- Think over what you want to say and organize your thoughts. Perhaps discuss the situation and what you propose to say and do with your colleague. Focus on what you want to come out of the contact with the parent. You might want to consult with the principal, your mentor, or a colleague for help and advice.
- Have your information and materials organized. Write down what you'll say.
- Make sure you're calm, collected, and prepared before any type of parental contact.

- Document your contact for your own records.
- Keep your principal informed of these contacts.

Have Parent–Teacher–Student Conferences

- Know when the conferences are scheduled.
- Remind parents of their conference times and express your eagerness to meet.
- Dress professionally.
- Think about what you specifically want to discuss concerning each student, and what work should be shared with the parent. Allow the student a voice in choosing work to share, as well as the actual sharing process.
- Start your conference on a positive note.
- Stick to the subject. There really isn't time to talk about personal experience or to stray too far from the purpose of the conference.
- Allow the students to speak—it's an opportunity for them to discuss what's taking place in the classroom, their strengths and weaknesses, and goals for the school year.
- Avoid discussing other children.
- Listen to what the parents have to say. To them, their child is unique and deserves to be given individual consideration, just as every other child in your class.
- Be ready, not only with suggestions for improvement, but with recommendations or procedures that might aid in improvement.
- Before you finish the conference, recap what you, the parents, and the child will do as a result of your

discussion. Be sure to give specific suggestions for ways to help the child with schoolwork, and encourage the parents to share their ideas.
- If you've agreed to further parental contacts, make sure to follow through.

Set Field Trip Guidelines

The Internet offers many options for virtual tours. While these can be taken in place of field trips, they can also be taken prior to the actual visit to provide students with a better understanding of the place and event, and allow them to ask higher-level questions both in advance and while on the trip. Community members are also an excellent resource to tap. The chance to speak with, listen to, and question these community experts gives students a broader perspective of the world outside the classroom. Guest speakers can be great leaders in a field trip experience.

Field trips are an excellent way to bring lessons to life. All students should be able to attend the trip unless there are concerns of safety for the student or the group if the student attends. At the high school level, trips can be extended over several days. It's up to the group leader to establish rules regarding what's acceptable to bring on the trip, room arrangements, chaperone assignments and duties, and overall behavior. Have parent–student meetings prior to the trip so expectations are clear and questions can be asked. As the coordinator, you have a huge responsibility and want

Connecting the Classroom to the Real World 65

parents to know that you understand the precious gift in your charge.

When you plan your trip, take into consideration the season and weather typical of the area you plan to visit. Plan well in advance so you have time to put together an enjoyable and meaningful trip. Mondays are not typically a good day to plan for a trip. Watch the school calendar for conflicts such as standardized testing for certain grades, concerts, plays, or athletic events. Once you've decided where and when to go, speak with your principal, department chair, and colleagues to verify there are no conflicts, and to invite them to join you. Then you can:

- Officially contact the place you'd like to visit. Secure the date and a cost per student. Determine the number of chaperones you'll need. Most establishments will allow a certain number of chaperones for free, and you pay for any beyond that number. If you feel you need additional chaperones, decide if you'll incorporate the cost of the chaperone into the students' overall fee or ask all chaperones to pay a fee that would cover the additional chaperone's entrance.
- Secure transportation for the date and time of your visit, both to and from the establishment. Most trips require bus transportation. Request a proposal from the company so that you can incorporate that amount into the overall fee of the field trip. Some field trips are walking trips, or parents can volunteer to drive.

There might be special forms for parent drivers due to liability of transporting students in personal vehicles. Check district policy regarding personal transportation regarding liability. Transportation in personal vehicles isn't usually recommended.
- Prepare a field trip permission slip in accordance with the guidelines of your district. Be sure to explicitly state where you'll be going, when, for what purpose (How does it tie into your curriculum?), how long you'll be gone, your return time, and the amount due. Then obtain a parent signature and date. If the trip extends through the lunch period, state the arrangements. This request should be sent a few weeks prior to your trip to give you time to follow-up with parents.
- Students aren't allowed to attend without the parental permission slip signed, so you need to make arrangements for any students who cannot go on the trip. If parents don't submit a signed permission slip it's often due to an inability to pay, an effort to punish the student, or mistrust of school personnel. You can contact the parents and discuss the situation openly. Explain the educational benefit of the trip. If finances are the problem, seek resources (PTA or community groups) that offer assistance, or you can pay for the student yourself.
- Place the field trip on the school's master calendar. Send a reminder to the parents approximately one week prior to the trip.

- A few days prior to the trip, finalize arrangements and be sure no last-minute changes have emerged with chaperones, transportation, or the establishment.
- Tie the trip to your curriculum. Be sure students understand the connection between the trip and the learning taking place in the classroom. You can create a guide book, questions, or a study guide for students. Follow-up projects, research, or writing activities can take place. Allow for student feedback once you've returned from the trip. Make notations as to what students found useful or interesting.
- Be sure to thank your chaperones! Communicating to the parents as to how the trip went and what the students viewed and learned is a great follow-up.

Put Suggestions in a Substitute Folder

Have a separate folder that remains in a location easily accessible by a substitute teacher. At minimum, the folder should include items such as:

- A class list for each class you teach
- Seating chart(s)
- A schedule that includes the times for specialists, lunch, and recess
- Attendance procedures
- Restroom, recess, lunch, and dismissal procedures
- Any duties they'll need to undertake on your behalf
- Fire drill, tornado, and other emergency procedures

- Classroom routines, such as where papers should be turned in, disbursement of materials, grouping, and leaders
- Location of lesson plans, worksheets, workbooks, teacher manuals, and any other materials the substitute will need throughout the day
- Any *crucial* student information such as diabetes, asthma, or allergies
- Names and locations of faculty who can answer questions
- Names of at least two responsible students (per class) who can provide assistance throughout the day
- A form letter in which the substitute can provide feedback of material covered and how the day went

Use Internet Resources

Appendix A includes some Internet resources colleagues and I have found particularly helpful. Please note that URLs (Internet addresses) sometimes change, so while this initial list will get you started, you will want to modify, add, and delete information as you work with sites and accumulate your personal favorites.

Appendix A

Internet Resources: Tools to Help You Teach

Note: These sites provide educational opportunities for children, but many of them contain advertisements and links to other websites. While the sites offer good, reliable information, I don't take responsibility for the content provided on these sites, nor their adherence to federal rules to protect children's privacy.

It's important to monitor students' online communication to ensure that they don't provide personally identifiable information. You should also preview these sites to become familiar with the information on the site, and bookmark or provide specific URLs to deter students from random surfing.

This isn't meant to be a comprehensive list, but rather a list of websites to get you started comfortably using and integrating technology in your classroom. Like education itself, educational websites cannot be pigeonholed into one content area. Therefore, sites are listed by where they *best* fit, but keep an open mind when searching for resources. Some sites for intermediate grades at the elementary level have been listed as resources to accommodate learners with special needs.

REFERENCE AND HOMEWORK HELPER WEBSITES

Check your state's Department of Public Instruction website. For example, Wisconsin's DPI site is http://www.dpi.state.wi.us and provides such information as state standards, school information, laws, and calendars.

A site of educational resources developed by a team of teachers: http://www.edhelper.com

Educational resources including clip art, lesson plans, and brain boosters: http://school.discovery.com

Tools and resources for the classroom: http://www.teacher.scholastic.com

Educational resources including lesson plans, professional development, and reading strategies: http://education-world.com

This site provides lesson plan ideas, student activities, resources, standards-based Web resources, and professional development opportunities: http://www.marcopolo-education.org/home.aspx or http://www.marcopolo-education.org/home.aspz

Lesson plan ideas available by content area: http://www.teachnet.com

Excellent resources such as lesson plans and rubrics, but many pop-ups and advertisements: http://www.LessonPlans.com

Teacher-tested resources for pre-K through adult education: http://ideas.wisconsin.edu

Housed in Florida, this site focuses on reading but provides links to additional teacher resources such as puzzles, rubrics, and quizzes: http://www.sunlink.ucf.edu

This site provides an explanation of standards and benchmarks in education: www.mcrel.org/standards-benchmarks/docs/process.asp

Fact Monster, which has received national recognition, offers reference materials, fun facts, and individualized homework assistance: http://www.factmonster.com

This site offers maps, facts, and descriptions of cities and countries around the world, with suggested links as additional resources and contact information for asking specific questions: http://www.worldatlas.com

Wikipedia is a free encyclopedia, offering several services from definitions to information on current events. Keep in mind, however, that the information is supplied (and modified) by users and as such isn't 100% reliable: http://www.wikipedia.org

Dictionary, references, grammar, usage, translator, and more: http://thesaurus.reference.com/

- Create your own puzzles in minutes! Includes crosswords, word finds, and other popular puzzles: www.puzzlemaker.com
- You don't have to re-create the wheel! This site offers many components to use in creating rubrics, as well as personalized rubrics: http://rubistar.4teachers.org/index.php
- From field trips to medication release forms, use these templates to create notes home in English or Spanish: http://casanotes.4teachers.org
- Similar to bookmarking your favorite Web pages, this site allows you to go beyond by organizing your sites for you. It also lets you to set up a daily routine and share information with others: http://www.backflip.com
- Assists educators with easy WebQuest style activities: http://pinetlibrary.com/index.php
- The Internet public library, a public service organization offered by the University of Michigan: http://www.ipl.org/div/news
- Kodak photo galleries for viewing, uploading, editing, and saving your personal photos: http://www.ofoto.com
- Photo galleries for viewing and purchasing, and the ability to upload your personal photos: http://dotphoto.com
- Edit photographs from digital images (website originates in England): http://www.photofiltre.com/
- Mac version to share photos and video clips: http://mac.com

Locates specific images as needed: http://images.google.com

Free program for recording and editing sound: http://audacity.sourceforge.net/

Now freeware instead of shareware, this program allows you to grab digital audio from CDs, not a soundcard, so it's excellent quality; make WAVs, MP3s, and more! http://www.audiograbber.com-us.net/

Library of Congress "American memory": http://memory.loc.gov/

Links to additional sites for lesson planning and educational resources: http://pic4learning.com

Schedules for public television along with resources and professional development opportunities: http://www.pbs.org

Search engine: http://www.kartoo.com

Publicly edited Web directory: http://www.dmoz.com

Exemplary practices in teaching Web evaluation: http://lib.nmsu.edu/staff/susabeck/checs98.html

Guides that children and teenagers can use to find specialized engines relating to their interests and school subjects: http://searchability.com/children.htm

K–12 teacher tools and curriculum support: http://www.bigchalk.com or http://www.proquestk12.com

Teacher guides available for 260 movies (subscription required): http://www.teachwithmovies.org/

SBC's website of lessons, WebQuests, and information for teachers and librarians: http://www.kn.pacbell.com/wired/fil/

- Create a Web page to house links, questions, directions, and explanations: http://www.eduhound.com/hotlist/
- Hosted by the Educational Technology Department of San Diego State University: http://webquest.sdsu.edu
- Examples of WebQuests: http://www.webquest.org
- Focuses on action research projects with students: http://www.hprtec.org
- Create notes for homework and class information and post it on the Web in seconds: http://schoolnotes.com
- Assists professional educators in planning, managing, and supporting online courses using online tools, resources, colleagues, and support to implement effective learning activities: http://www.tappedin.org
- Assists educators in addressing common technology integration questions by providing practical, online resources and activities: http://eduscapes.com/tap/
- The Educational Technology Journal published by Jamie McKenzie, EdD: http://www.fno.org/
- The George Lucas Educational Foundation hosts Edutopia: The New World of Learning, which includes professional articles, topics of interest, and professional development opportunities: http://www.glef.org
- Translation from English to other languages including Spanish at no cost: http://www.freetranslation.com

MULTIPLE AREAS OF LEARNING

From the United Kingdom, this site offers activities for age groups 4-16 in many content areas. Students choose the appropriate age level, the type of content they want to practice, and they are given a selection of activities. There is also a teacher resource page with helpful information and links: http://www.bbc.co.uk/schools/

Innovative teaching materials for teachers, useful and enjoyable resources for students, and advice for parents on how to help their children enjoy learning and excel in school. The site is constantly reviewed for educational relevance by practicing classroom teachers at each level: elementary, middle, and high school: http://school.discovery.com

Information on the educational television shows broadcast by PBS. PBS Kids websites include at-home activities, lesson plans, educational guides, and tips for parents and teachers, as well as activities and games based on their television shows: www.pbskids.org

Kid's Education Place, produced by Houghton Mifflin Company, offers children's games and activities in math, reading, language arts, social studies, and more: http://www.eduplace.com/kids/

The site offers more than 800 interactive games and activities for preschool through the 6th grade that are fun and easy to use: http://www.funschool.com/

MATH

Tutorials for higher mathematics: http://www.sos-math.com

A real-time math resource: http://www.planetmath.org

Math timed tests completed on the computer, with immediate feedback: http://www.scugog-net.com/room108/MadMath/mmm.htm

Math problems, games, and articles: http://www.nrich.maths.org.uk

Create games, activities, flash cards, scavenger hunts, and more (subscription necessary): http://www.quia.com/dir/math

Multiplication, where clicking on the correct answer continues the story: http://schoolcentral.com/willoughby5/

Multiplication activities: http://www.multiplication.com/internet_games.htm

Multiplication baseball: http://www.prongo.com/math/

Site includes some free drill games; other resources available with membership fee: http://www.edu4kids.com/index.php

A variety of math activities: http://www.aplusmath.com

AAA math: basic math skills, interactive practice, explanations, and challenge games for kindergarten through eighth grade. These pages illustrate and provide interactive exercises and problems and contain a series of basic math lessons. A resource that can be used by math students in formal elementary education math classes, home schooling, and elsewhere: http://www.aaamath.com/

Math games and explanations for students from age three to high school: http://www.coolmath.com/home.htm

SCIENCE

This site provides excellent resources for kids, students. and teachers: homework help, Internet resources, multimedia, and contact information for grades K–4, 5–8, and 9–12: http://www.nasa.gov/home/index.html

Grand explanation of the Shedd Aquarium: http://www.sheddnet.org

From science projects to games, these sites have something for all ages: http://www.sandiegozoo and http://www.planetpals.com/weather.html

This site is an excellent resource for exploring different areas of biology. Contacts are available so students can ask specific questions related to the field of biology: http://biology.usgs.gov/pub_aff/usgsbio.html

This site provides quizzes on different areas of the anatomy: www.msjensen.gen.umn.edu/webanatomy/

This site offers biological and biochemical lessons and tutorials: www.biology.arizona.edu/cell_bio/cell_bio.html

Jurassic Park's Dinosaur Site, interactive and informational: http://www.jpinstitute.com

Animal Diversity Web, an online database of animal natural history, distribution, classification, and conservation biology at the University of Michigan: http://animaldiversity.ummz.umich.edu/site/index.html

This child-friendly site offerering interactive information on careers, animal care, and general information about animals, with very nice graphics. Operated by the American Society for the Prevention of Cruelty to Animals: http://www.animaland.org/

Freddo Frog's Pond on the Web, which provides a discussion on environmental and safety issues: http://www.greenweb.com.au/freddo/index.html

Comprehensive site about the world of insects, ranging from identification to bug cuisine: http://www.insectclopedia.com/

Defenders of Wildlife is dedicated to the protection of all native wild animals and plants in their natural communities, focusing its programs on what scientists consider two of the most serious environmental threats to the planet: the accelerating rate of extinction of species and associated loss of biological diversity, and habitat alteration and destruction: http://www.kidsplanet.org/

National Wildlife Federation is the nation's largest and oldest protector of wildlife. The Kids Page features articles in English and Spanish from Ranger Rick, the environmental magazine for children; a homework help section; and briefings on issues such as the wetlands, endangered animals, water quality, and more: http://www.nwf.org/kids/

Tips for taking care of your pet from the American Animal Hospital Association. Lets you find the pet hospital nearest to where you live: http://www.healthypet.com/Library/index.html#caretips

Sea World/Busch Gardens animal information database is designed especially for students and teachers and the Sea World/Busch Gardens animal information database brings the world of wildlife to classrooms! Download cool animal facts, teacher's guides, quizzes, activities . . . even check out live animal cams! http://www.seaworld.org

Motion, inertia, roller coasters, and virtual dissections: http://everyschool.org/u/BretHarte/zpeters/ratz.html

Dozens of atmospheric, oceanic, geophysical, and space science sites: http://www.cv.nrao.edu/fits/www/yp_earth.html

Yahoo listing of science- and astronomy-related topics: http://www.yahoo.com/Science/Astronomy/

Virtual Dissections

Procedure for frog dissection and identification of organs: http://curry.edschool.virginia.edu/go/frog/

Dissection of a cow's eye: http://www.exploratorium.edu/learning_studio/cow_eye/index.html

Dissection of a sheep's brain: http://academic.uofs.edu/department/psych/sheep/

Dissection of an earthworm: http://plato.acadiau.ca/courses/biol/macdougall/calgary/Worm/Beginwm.htm

Dissection of a fetal pig: http://mail.fkchs.sad27.k12.me.us/fkchs/vpig/

Dissection of a VPD: http://www.whitman.edu/offices_departments/biology/vpd/main.html

Dissection of a clam: http://BioG-101-104.bio.cornell.edu/BioG101_104/tutorials/animals/clam.html

Dissection of a squid: http://BioG-101-104.bio.cornell.edu/BioG101_104/tutorials/animals/squid.html

Dissection of a cat: http://www.bhs.berkeley.k12.ca.us/departments/Science/anatomy/cat/index.html

Dissection of a cockroach: http://everest.ento.vt.edu/~carroll/insect_video_dissection.html

Dissection of a rat: http://www.umanitoba.ca/faculties/science/biological_sciences/lab15/

SOCIAL STUDIES

Answers questions regarding geography, maps, travel, and flags: http://www.graphicmaps.com/clipart.hrm

Research for pictures, articles, maps, and more. Includes MapMachine to locate a city or country: http://www.nationalgeographic.com/kids/

Pictures and facts about each of our presidents: http://www.americanpresidents.org

Provides information on America's history. Students can play games that have to do with the states and the history of the U.S.: http://www.americaslibrary.gov/cgi.bin/page.cgi

A direct link to the Smithsonian Institution, or our "nation's attic": http://www.si.edu/

Provides links to federal kids' sites along with some of the best sites from other organizations grouped by subject. This site also has different categories such as arts, careers, computers, geography, health, history, and music and offers links to other sites: http://www.kids.gov/

Time for Kids Online, offered at levels K–6. Children can keep up with the news written on their grade level: http://www.timeforkids.com/TFK/

Presidents

http://www.americanpresidents.org
http://www.whitehouse.gov
http://www.presidentsusa.net
http://gi.grolier.com/presidents/

50 States

http://www.theus50.com
http://www.infoplease.com/states.html
http://factfinder.census.gov/home/en/kids/funfacts/funfacts.html
http://www.netstate.com/states/index.html
http://www.50states.com

History of Wisconsin

http://www.wisconsin.gov/state/core/wisconsin_state_capitol_tour.html
http://www.50states.com/wisconsin.htm

http://www.wisconsinhistory.org/turningpoints/subtopic.asp?tid=1
http://agency.travelwisconsin.com/PR/Tourism_Facts/Facts.shtm
http://www.infoplease.com/ipa/A0108291.html
http://www.wisconsin.gov/state/core/wisconsin_state_capitol_tour.html
http://www.wisconsinhistory.org/turningpoints/subtopic.asp?tid=1

LANGUAGE ARTS

http://eleaston.com
www.teenwriting.about.com/od/writingpoetry
http://flyingarts.net/workshops/basics/
http://www.shadowpoetry.com/resources/wip/types.html
http://www.rhymer.com/

CREATIVITY AND EDUCATIONAL GAMES

Chess Kids. Learn to play chess with interactive lessons, quizzes, games, and puzzles: http://www.chesskids.com

Kid Wizard is a fun, educational place where kids ages six to twelve can play games, solve mysteries, make decisions in the interactive story, and find out that magic does exist: http://www.kidwizard.com/

Kids Hub is a free online interactive learning center for elementary school students. It features fun educational games, puzzles, and quizzes: http://kidshub.org/kids/kids.cfm

VIRTUAL TOURS

http://www.senate.gov/vtour
http://www.virtualfreesites.com/tours.html
http://www.virtualfreesites.com/us.government.html
http://www.chinavista.com/travel/virtualtours.html
http://www.louvre.fr/llv/commun/home_flash.jsp?bmLocale=en
http://archpropplan.auckland.ac.nz/virtualtour/

ART

http://www.edbydesign.com/art/artists.html
http://www.moma.org/destination/
http://www.scituate.k12.ma.us/docent/
www.artlex.com
www.thewaichulisstudio.net
www.metmuseum.org
www.moma.org
www.mam.org.

MUSIC

http://www.isd77.k12.mn.us/resources/staffpages/shirk/k12.music.html

http://musiced.about.com/
http://www.creatingmusic.com
http://www.sphinxkids.org
http://www.edu-cyberpg.com/Music/m_sites2.html
http://datadragon.com/education/

LISTINGS OF OTHER WEBSITES

Provides an extensive list of educational and fun websites in many different areas of learning: http://www.busyteacherscafe.com/kidsite.htm#General%20Websites

Just for Kids. Provides links to animals, dinosaurs, educational games, "just for fun," magazines and news, science and museums, space, sports, travel, TV, radio, and music: http://www.eagle.ca/~matink/kids.html

Association for Library Service to Children, which links to educational sites on animals, the arts, history and biographies, literature and language, math and computers, social sciences, and science: http://www.ala.org/ala/alsc/greatwebsites/greatwebsiteskids.htm

The mission of Cyberkids is to provide a voice for young people on the Internet by publishing original creative work by kids ages 7 to 12: http://www.cyberkids.com/index.html

Appendix B

Parent–Teacher Communication

LETTER 1

August 2006
Dear Students and Parents:

Welcome to the new school year! My name is Mrs. Strike and I teach Freshman English and Composition. Some of the books we will read this year are *Romeo and Juliet* and *To Kill a Mockingbird*. There will also be opportunities for you to choose which book you would like to read. We will use literary circles. I am the forensics coach, and hope to see many of you participate. I also host a breakfast book club before school on Tuesdays from 7:15 to 7:45.

You will maintain a journal in my class, so you will need a spiral notebook or notebook paper in a binder. Always bring your journal, the book we are reading, and something to write with to class. Be on time and ready to work!

I am anxious to get started and look forward to our school year together.
Sincerely,
Mrs. Strike

LETTER 2

September 2006
Dear Parents:

On Tuesday, September 19, I hope that you can join us at Park High School for Open House from 6:00 to 8:00 in the evening. During that time, your son/daughter can bring you through a shortened version of his/her schedule and show you some of his/her work. While I would like to discuss your child's progress with you, please understand that this is not the appropriate forum to do so. If you have concerns, please feel free to contact me via telephone at 555-1212 or e-mail at kstrike@parkhs.k12.wi.us to ensure we have the privacy and the dedicated time to address your questions or concerns. If I have concerns about your child, I have already contacted you. Parent–teacher–student conferences will be held November 15–17, and I will be meeting with each of you during this time. I will have a sign-up sheet available at the open house for your convenience.

I look forward to meeting you. Please feel free to contact me with any questions.
Sincerely,
Mrs. Strike

LETTER 3

October 21

Dear Parents:

Our students have completed reading *Romeo and Juliet* and will be attending the play at the Theatre Guild on Wednesday, November 8. The students will miss their morning classes and will need to make up their work. We will be back in the building in time for the first lunch. The cost of the field trip is $9.50, which includes the cost of admission and transportation. I am in need of at least three parent chaperones to attend the trip with us.

Please complete and sign the form below and return it to school by Wednesday, November 1.

Thank you,

Mrs. Strike

I, _____, give my permission for my son/daughter, _____, to attend the field trip to the Theatre Guild on Wednesday, November 8. I understand that my child will miss morning classes and will need to make up this work on his/her own.

_____

Parent Signature   Date   Emergency/Work Number

_____ I have included $9.50 to cover the admission and transportation for the field trip.

_____ I am interested in chaperoning the trip. I can be reached at _____.

LETTER 4

November 2006

Dear Parents:

Parent–teacher–student conferences are right around the corner. I am excitedly waiting for the opportunity to discuss your child's progress with you. These conferences allow for a three-way conversation to take place. This is important for several reasons. First, you are your child's best teacher and know your child best. You know your child's strengths and weaknesses. Second, your child is an active participant in this partnership. Without his or her effort and attention, learning would not take place. Therefore, it is important to hear your child's perspective of how things are going, what is working, and what needs work. Finally, I have the privilege of teaching your child this year. For us to best use our short time together, I have a few questions I would like you to answer. By returning the completed sheet prior to the conference, it will allow me to see if you have specific questions or concerns and gather additional information for you. I have attached the sheet for your convenience.

Your conference time is scheduled for 3:20–3:40 on Thursday, November 16. You child is the STAR! Please be sure he or she attends with you. Arrangements should be made for siblings. I will have an activity table set up in the hallway for children to color, read, and build.

If you need to change your appointment, please contact me at 555-1212 to make other arrangements.

I look forward to our meeting,

Mrs. Strike

LETTER 5

December 12, 2006

Dear Parents:

Just a reminder that our Holiday Concert is coming up on Tuesday, December 19. Students should report to their homerooms at 6:45. The concert will begin at 7:00, and last approximately 1.5 hours. Attire is dark pants and a light shirt, or attire that reflects the holiday spirit. We hope that you will join us for this special event.

Happy Holidays!

Mrs. Strike

CONFERENCE QUESTIONS

1. What my son/daughter likes best about school is:

   _____
   _____
   _____

2. What my son/daughter likes least about school is:

   _____
   _____
   _____

3. Some questions I'd like to ask are:

_____
_____
_____

4. Some concerns I have are:

_____
_____
_____

5. At home my son/daughter enjoys _____ and displays behaviors such as: _____. Is this consistent with how he/she acts at school?

6. Some friends that my son/daughter hang around with are _____. Are these relationships evident here at school? _____

7. Four words I would use to describe my child are:

_____
_____
_____

8. Four words my child uses to describe him/herself are:

_____
_____
_____

9. Are there any inconsistencies that I should be aware of, such as truancies, absences, or changes in moods or behavior?

_____
_____
_____

FROM THE DESK OF _____
WEEK OF _____

Lab Science

_____
_____
_____

Biology

_____
_____
_____

Earth Science

_____
_____
_____

Special Events

_____
_____
_____

BEHAVIOR REPORT FOR _____

Subject	**How I Think I Did**	**How the Teacher Thinks I Did**
Reading		
Math		
Specialist		

Parent Signature: _____

Appendix B

PROGRESS REPORT FOR _____

Date: _____

Task   **Yes**   **No**

I raised my hand to speak
I stayed in my seat
I remained on task
I completed my work (well done and on time)
I was a good listener

Comments: _____
_____
_____

Missing Work:

_____
_____
_____

Parent Signature:_____

PROGRESS REPORT FOR _____

Date: _____

Class	Teacher comments	Grade	Missing Work	Work Habits in Class
Math				
English				
Spelling/ Vocab.				
Reading/ Lit.				
Soc. Studies				
Science				
Specialist				

Parent Signature: _____

REFERENCES

Diffily, D., and Sessman, C. (2004). *Teaching Effective Classroom Routines.* New York, NY: Scholastic, Inc.

Gavaert, C. (2006). *Using Free Software in the Waukesha Public Schools.* Milwaukee, WI. Milwaukee Educational Computing Association (MECA) newsletter V15 N3 P3.

Learning Books. (1987). *Classroom Management.* Bethlehem Pike, Springfield, PA: Springhouse Corporation.

Ormrod, J. E. (2006). *Educational psychology: Developing learners* (5th ed.). Upper Saddle River, NJ: Pearson Education.

Wisconsin Education Association Council (WEAC). (1989). *The Beginning Teacher Handbook: A Book of Firsts.* Madison, WI. Developed by the WEAC Instruction and Professional Development Committee (IPD).

http://www.competitionmaster.com/pages/career/professionalism.html (retrieved 12/27/05).

http://www.goalsinstitute.com/professionalism-g.html?gclid=CI6_sJWwnYICFQ7hIgodCibuDQ (retrieved 12/27/05).

About the Author

Kimberly T. Strike (doctorate, Marquette University) has been an administrator, teacher, educational consultant, and guest speaker. Her experience crosses public, private, and parochial sectors; urban and rural districts; and adult and youth education. She was an educational ambassador to China (Datong and Beijing) in 2005 and a missionary to Russia (Ivanovo and Moscow) in 2006.